# Way of Whiteness

Other books by
Wendy Barker

Poetry:
*Winter Chickens*
*Let the Ice Speak*
*Eve Remembers*

Criticism:
*Lunacy of Light: Emily Dickinson*
*and the Experience of Metaphor*

Edited:
(with Sandra M. Gilbert)
*The House Is Made of Poetry:*
*The Art of Ruth Stone*

# Way of Whiteness

**Wendy Barker**

San Antonio, Texas
2000

*Way of Whiteness* © 2000 by Wendy Barker

First printing

ISBN: 0-930324-55-2

Wings Press
627 E. Guenther
San Antonio, Texas 78210
Ph/fax: (210) 271-7805

On-line catalogue and ordering:
www.wingspress.com

Cover photograph, *Attempting Ascension*,
by Susan Lirakis Nicolay

# CONTENTS

## III    WAY OF WHITENESS

*for Jeannine Keenan and Sherry McKinney*

# Way of Whiteness

# I

# CEREMONIES

# Taking a Language

I hear them, my husband and son, practicing
sounds in French I have almost forgotten.

*La famille. Leurs mots. Deux, trois.*
I don't join them. I have enough to do.

Every day the same steps to another day,
blinds pulled until the metal slats slide

to a tidy line above the window.
One bed made at a time, one side at a time,

my arms not long enough
to cross the space between us.

I have grown impatient with slow
progressions—with touch that may not lead

to love, the time it takes
to wait for the ends of sentences—and yet

in high school we couldn't even complete
a simple Latin sentence as

we followed our teacher through each
person of a verb, singular, *amo, amas, amat,*

plural, *amamus, amatis, amant,* present, past,
future perfect conditional.   We didn't know

where we were going.  I had no idea
in that class I would meet the boy whose

tongue was the first to reach to mine.
It took our entire sophomore year to translate

Caesar's accounts of the individual
customs of the tribes, the *Helvetii, Belgae.*

All Gaul was divided into single parts.
Evenings facing a new grammar,

nights in the back seat of a Chevy,
years before we were proficient

in the language of the country of love,
before we had entered

a French cathedral, to find the pattern
of small stones lined

to lead the devout to a state of prayer.  Placing
the left foot one stone in front of the right,

heel and sole on stone,
one does not notice the rose window above

until, with an accidental glance,
light explodes, wheeling

spheres within spheres,
mother, child, man, innumerable

facets of glass. I had forgotten.
And below, a smaller window

where shoemakers bend to their task,
piercing the tiny holes lined in a row

to draw the laces through,
one, two at a time.

# Matter of Singing

*Why – do they shut me out of Heaven?*
*Did I sing – too loud?*
                    – Emily Dickinson

*Her voice was ever soft, gentle, and low,*
*an excellent thing in woman.*
                    – King Lear

I read in the papers that a woman
has been arrested because she sang
again at mass, the voice she says
of an angel who comes to her.
In fourth grade, on the school bus,
the driver told me to hush, no singing
on the way to school.  Fall mornings
cooling, pyracantha berries
reddening.  I had been happy.

                    ✠

Once in a sudden summer rain,
he had to put his Healey's top up,
for the first time heard my singing.
Said to stop.  Every day he taught
people how not to sing like that,
didn't want to be reminded.  The way
most women sound when they sing.

Too much breath.  The smoldering
inside a throat, of notes wanting.

☩

At the Vienna Volksoper, Mozart's
Queen of the Night floats to the stage
a cluster of stars, notes so high
they lift beyond the carved ceiling,
ranges of the Danube, the Alps.
In the last act, she has fallen to
the floor, taken from the others'
reunion.  We have lost her
high notes rising, resisting limits.

☩

The voice that woke me in Berkeley.
Someone playing a flute, piercing
the night till I could not sleep.
A blanket in the hills, eucalyptus
rustling above us, their brown bells
around us, breath merging into breath
as he asked if I wanted to
sing again, again. Impossible not to.

## Some Days the Only

horse in the field is the dull gray one.
Days when a husband of many years sags

into the upholstery of what might have been.
Days when I stare beyond his head

to relive the moments I have said no
to say yes to the familiar, keep intact

the tidiness of cupboards.  For years
I have been sweeping, vacuuming dust

that refuses to settle.  Even the grasses
of the field have turned drab as the horse,

beyond whose bulk may be nothing, not even
a gate leading to winter ground.

# Of Mice and Men

1.

We are setting traps, packs of D-Con.  Overrun
again by mice, rolls of paper towels chewed through,
soft nests of leavings
over the floor, bits of bird seed,
clumps of the litter left after the hamster died.

So old he could no longer move to his water.
You drowned him, our fourth hamster.
We decided not to replace him.

We set bait in every kitchen cupboard.
By the third morning there are no more sounds
of scuttling.

I sweep the floors of the closets, clean
down to the boards.


2.

We've been here before.  The loyalty of parents
when their kids perform.  High school plays
can have their moments, between the slow, jerky
changes of scenes.

This time we don't recognize our son,
bent with the weight of eighty years,
voice older than my father's before he died.
It's not so much the wig, the fragile silver hair,
as it is the tremor in the voice, the hand.

We have read the novel, think we know
what we are in for.
But when our son repeats
to the ranch hands who want to kill his old dog,
"I've had him from a pup," and when
the dog is shot and David's back jerks,
when we see him an old man turning to the wall
in a narrow bed before an audience of hundreds,
I am gripped by something harsher than stage lights,
darker than the farthest corner of this auditorium
after everyone has gone home.

In the glare of the lobby, I can't find him
among the kids receiving hugs and flowers.
Can this be my son?  I ask him
to pull off the wisps of beard, I have to touch
his neck, his cheek, I have to know
it is still his young skin
under that white hair.

Driving home without him, we don't talk,
I lean on you the way I used to.
We thought we knew what we were in for.
We used to quote from Steinbeck's novel: I would say

"Tell me about the rabbits," and you would read
from Rodale's *Raising Small Livestock*.
You said we would build the cages
so the rabbits could be kept clean, dry,
well-fed, could tend their young.


3.


That fall morning we found
David out by the pool kneeling
over the edge, over a field mouse
he was lifting from the hose that floats on the water.
The mouse must have fallen in during the night,
must have swum to the hose and clung
until our son woke
to find him trembling.

We dried his fur with a garden glove,
carried him to a hollow in the grasses, brought
bird seed from the house, and left him alone.

At first when we went to check, he was still there.
But later, when we went again, there was only
the wind sweeping the grass.

## Stylist

He's been cutting my hair for six months now,
takes over an hour for a blunt cut
that I know could take half the time

but that would shorten the show.
Already I need him, one of his dependent
women who, he tells me between drags on his cigarette,

are much older than he, thank god, even though he is,
this very weekend (his booth bulging orchids and purple
ribbons), turning, god forbid, 36.

He would die cutting the heads of girls, would know he was ancient.
He stops, drops the scissors on the table, lights a new cigarette,
asks me, would I like to know the truth

about why he decided, after 4 wives and 2000 women, on men?
Because he watched them age, he said, and there's no
comparison, he said, moving in with the blades.

He liked the big ones, the ones with the huge cabangas,
and honey, they just don't hold up.  Thank god
he found Joel, they're a perfect pair,

Joel's ten years younger,
a devoted husband, they've been faithful
for six years, Joel even makes their clothes.

He tells me to buy a teddy.
Four inch spike heels, we professional women have no idea
how sexy we could look, tottering around.

I should get myself some,
and I should get myself immortalized,
he has a friend who does portraits,

discreet, tasteful poses on a chaise,
my husband would love it.
Better do it soon, shouldn't wait much longer.

# Color Analysis

A fiftieth birthday gift.
Swatches of fabric held to my face.
I am a "Summer," am told
I mustn't wear winter, clear, sharp
colors of gems: rubies, sapphires, emeralds,
onyx. No mining black rock
for me. No snow, no black
branches of a naked tree.
Nothing too strong, definite,
I am semi-precious: amethyst, aquamarine, colors
of sky. I am probably an air sign.
Think of breezes, says my color counselor.

Then what are these wiry black
hairs that sprout in my blond eyebrows?
The dots of scarlet on my legs?
Pure white patches on my arms,
rents in the fabric of so many summer tans.
Flecks and cracks of shadow and blood
weaving now, my body.

I am told to have nothing to do
with the press of bright yellow, liquid greens
that rush the landscape in April and May.

No ooze of apricot.
Autumn would overwhelm me.
Crush of dark berry fruit.
Brown. I must not even think
of earth. Have nothing to do with rust.

To what season, then, am I linked,
apparently forever, floating
rootless on pale air? Am I simply
to sway here on wisps of gray,
pale cloud, a little gasp of pink,
fading lavender as the sun's face sinks?

# The Bottom

We knew she had lost it when she began to lift
the skirts of her silky I. Magnin dresses, twitch
her girdle side to side before she reached
the bathroom at the end of the downstairs hall.
They trembled as they moved beyond our vision,
largest parts of Grandma's little body, two great
flabby moons, drooping over her dropped girdle,
loosened garters, stockings wisping her thighs.
We tried to look the other way. Impossible

years later when our old friend the oncologist,
opera buff, beaming above the table's silver
at his fortieth, stood up at his place as if
to toast us all, then turned and dropped his
slacks right there, holding still so we could see
the small wisps of hair that shaded his two round
nippleless bottom breasts. I couldn't keep from
laughing—so hard my sides hurt. But I had no idea
what it was he offered, what he gave. Recently

mine have begun to drift below, beyond their
laundered, elasticized borders. A private
continental drift, as if the body is trying to
move beyond the narrow shape of itself, as if

each buttock were an outsized protoplasmic cell
dividing into a clump of overblown roses, giant
marshmallows held too long over the fire.
As if the body has become a low cloud building,
heavier and heavier with its own held weight.
The effort to keep it all together. The urge
of the body to move beyond geometry.

## Olympic Trials

Hip to hip last night we watched the Summer Olympics
on TV, the middle-aged Russian heavy-weight lifter
who came back after 12 years to win the silver.
Later, they showed the terrorists' slaughter
of the Israeli team in Munich, twenty years ago.
The pain of setting foot on that ground again.
The summer we lived in someone else's house
trying to rebuild our 10-year-old marriage.
Finding out about each other's lovers.
Separate rooms in the Phoenix heat.
Learning to touch again.

Tonight the divers are careening
heels over head, arms extended
to the deep water.  One of the divers
opens his body too early, slams flat
against the surface.  He had been close
to a bronze, now he has lost his standing.
When he steps from the pool, his back is
the color of exposed muscle.  What is it
you and I keep trying to say to each other?
From the platform the water looks so far down.
After his next dive, a perfect slice straight through,
the crowd goes wild.  Their palms must sting, burn
from such clapping, longer and harder than
for the 16-year-old who takes the gold.

# On the Subject of Jackets

Toward the last, my father asked for his tweed
jacket, described the tie, the striped shirt
he wanted to wear to the hospital, not knowing

he would be strapped to a gurney, dressed
only in a short cotton gown for the winding
ambulance ride on New Hampshire roads

across the river. I followed in the car with
my mother, snug behind the wheel, sun through
the windshield. A thermos of tea beside us.

He asked for his jacket in the voice he had used
to a secretary on the other side of his polished desk.
People signed their names to his words.

Today you tell me your grandfather, seventy years
ranching in the Texas hills, is dying. Matter of fact,
you say when it happens you won't know who you are.

Clean blue of a New England September sky
as my mother and I pushed through the glass
entrance from the shop-lined street where

I decided to buy a jacket. Soft, same blue
as the skirt I wore that he had touched,
saying, "Pretty, this is pretty."

Every morning I pressed that skirt,
stroked the iron over the blue
cloth of the jacket, color of his eyes.

Wore it when I walked into his room
unable to talk because he couldn't.
For weeks, the jacket covered me

as I met my classes. And then one afternoon,
I left it in the room where I met you
that fall my father died. Your blue eyes, like his.

You talk now of the way your grandfather
wielded a knife for castrating calves.
The jacket's cloth was smooth from all that ironing.

I never got it back. I have nothing left to prepare you
for the cold, except what I cannot give. Stroking
of skin on skin. The clothes we can never wear.

# Ceremonies for the Dead

1.

I have never learned the right way
to say goodbye.  Friends drift
to another section of the river
and by the time you look up from your own
thrashings to stay afloat, they are so far
even a shrill call won't find them.
All you can do is keep up with the current
that pushes you cold on to the river's mouth.

2.

When that student died to me he was holding
a flask of olive oil in his hand, his gift.
In the car, we said goodbye
to the people we had been.
I don't know who he is now.
I don't know who either of us is becoming.

3.

So little warning.  The grizzled friend
whose jokes we are still trying to retell
died after successful prostate surgery.
In Tuscany together we had all walked
through the Etruscan museum, studying
cinerary urns.  Who had fashioned the statuary
of the dead whose cinders lived inside?
Who decided the shape that determined
how one would be remembered?
A man reclining, leaning on an elbow,
other arm pointing to a ship.
Was this the gesture he wanted us to know?
Perhaps, instead, it would have been
a kiss on his daughter's forehead.


4.

It takes four handwritten pages
for my old friend from college to say
she is ending our friendship
and I am not to write back.
She must be no longer
the woman I have loved and yet
I will do as she says, I will not write.
But neither will I destroy her letter
and when her birthday comes round
again, I will not forget.

5.

This is what it comes to.  The air that passes
in and out of pores until it is no longer
your air or mine, simply the woven threads
of our lungs' shuttles, all of our
heavings, exchanged.  Whose is whose?
To continue the small regular breathings.
There will be no cinerary urn.
No one will be commissioned.

# II

# ANNUNCIATIONS

# Generation

The eggs that have dropped alone into the womb
over the years, hundreds
of thousands of sperm that have shrivelled
in their struggle up through the soft plush
to reach the great sun, ovum, be the one
who makes the successful stab at the vast arc,
pierces the envelope.
              And the ovum, embracing
the one who finds her, the sleek
one who pillows himself so surprisingly
determined under her covers, this tiny whipping
pulse that plunges upriver
to reach her or die, she is so moved
she lets him
break her tight closed circle,
wave and rock through her entirety
until she finds herself multiplied, two
in one, four of two, eight from four,
till a face takes shape, fingers
separate from the palm of a hand
that assumes a shape like the hand of
the woman who surrounds all this,

who thinks she has caused all this
while a hand strokes her abdomen, her hand
pulls him down to her again
                    and again not thinking
of all the eggs yet stored
that will never be opened, never have
the chance to lose
whatever it was they had been.

# In Venice the Travellers

lighten, they have left behind
London, rectangular landmarks,
neighborhoods of the famous

novelists, upholstered homes
of Dickens, Carlyle.  Have left
the clacking of their jet-lagged heels

dragging through Bloomsbury, through
the floors of the National Portrait
Gallery, lines of public faces.

Ready for Venice, for water
that lures them over bridges
whose names they can't pronounce,

lures them into shops glistening
with glass swirled into vines, petals, swans
shimmering like the canals

that dazzle silver flowers in the afternoon,
the water that blazes, crackles gold
blood loosed to the tide

in the evening.  When they stop, catch
their breath, they stare down into the chasm
lengthening shadow that shapes

the under arch of a bridge
and their eyes fix on the water
beneath.  Nothing is reflected.

They no longer remember
what they had forgotten to tell
the neighbor who is watching the house,

no longer notice who stands next to them
on the bridge, or the moment
they let drop with no splash

their memory of maps,
the way to go back,
the shapes of their own faces.

# Ithaca, on the Landing

How was it Penelope waited
upstairs all those years,
before he finally

found his way back?
Every night unravelling the weave,
her fear of fixing to the wrong one

knitting her nerves.
But the wool kept the shape of the warp,
she could not straighten the strands

after so many nights.
All day weaving with more and more
wrinkled skeins, all night pulling out

threads with her fingers,
all that winding
and rewinding, back and forth

across the loom after breakfast,
the sound of the soft
contact betwen wool and wood,

the rhythm, meshing
color upon color, and then
at night the whole thing in reverse,

everything pulled apart
until blue and silver
strands turned dull, lost their sheen.

Sometimes she would stop, try to see
beyond the window's flat shadow.
She could not know him

through that space, she could not know
who he would be
becoming in those years

of sailing, slipping into fern-
lined coves, dashing his prow
against headlands so splashed

with sun and spume
that at first he couldn't even tell
who lived there.

And who was it
he would come home to
after all her nights unravelling?

Sometimes during those
unfinished years, sometimes under
the weight of a blunt moon,

she thought she heard music,
one of the men on the ground floor
singing, softly singing,

and once she leaned down
over the upstairs landing to see
how they lounged in her chairs.

She travelled their faces:
not brutes, not swine, but men,
beards curled across their cheeks.

Some young, smooth
as the rubbed wood of her loom.
And the lean one with the flute,

long thighs relaxed
in sleep, smiling in his sleep.
What if, at night,

she left her weaving alone?
Let it grow, become whole?
What might the tapestry become

if she stopped saying no
over and over, refusing
the downstairs of her own house?

# Facing Masks

Venice closes down early. By ten
the alleys have blackened, so narrow
the travellers walk single file.

Magic how they emerge
into the lighted campo, face
the mask maker's shop where they had

lingered that afternoon.
Hundreds of masks, their eyes
open to a dark wall,

silky, gleaming faces
of queens, demons, fish.
One of them, enormous:

silver and gold, a sliver of moon
kissing a full round sun
billowing flames like a halo.

One of the travellers
had opened her purse,
*bellissimo*, she had said.

But not like her to desire
something so big, expensive,
difficult to pack.

Face to face she stood
with the man who made the masks
and told him *no, grazie, no.*

                    Late that night
the moon will silver
the shutters of her window.
She will not sleep but think

back over a dozen canals, shadowed
bridges, and her desire will rise
for the mask,
                    the mask maker.

His faces, hundreds
of colors, some with lines
like blood running through them,

some made of lace, delicate
as expensive underthings.
The gold and silver one,

sun and moon, embracing.
What kind of man is he
to know so many faces?

He would live behind the front
of his shop. Halls would stretch
back into rooms opening

to a balcony, to the dark
water. Cushions on a tile floor.
Pillowy chairs, he might even have

one chair for every mask
he has ever made. If she could
let herself down

in them. Take her time.
And if he—with his long fingers—
would loosen

all her old tight masks,
take them off. What would she do,
then, with such lightness,

her own sun and moon
rising liquid to the zenith
of the sky she is breathing, he is

breathing her hair
into feathers, tendrils, flames that uncurl,
burst the lines of her face.

# The Face That

She didn't launch anything.  Only herself,
when she left Menelaus, snoring, every
couple of weeks grabbing her, poking
a jagged fingernail, stinking ale.  Always
she had known, from her swan-feather youth,
she herself made only half a broken egg.

The loveliness of the one who had come
for her.  Black eyes like meteors, peonies.
He didn't say he was a prince.  Come down
from the high mountains where he had slept
with the wind that swept through the trees
like desire, like the way she wanted him.

So they left.  That simple.  She chose to
leave the stale place that kept women inside,
kept tedious track of children's last names.
She remembered the stories of the old women
who spoke from their tapestries of a time
when it hadn't mattered who fathered a child

as long as there had been delight.  After their
first pleasure, couldn't they have returned
to the mountain, arms around arms, unnoticed?
Couldn't they have launched a new people,
lovely as black and white swans, fire-red
shooting stars, whole unbroken eggs?

# The Judgment: Aphrodite Speaks


As usual, unless it involved masquerading, cross-dressing
as a bird or bull, old Zeus avoided conflict. Let someone else
decide which way we'll move on it, he said. You're all
coming at me at once. I can only do one thing at a time.

It wasn't any of us who wanted a decision, it was Eris
who always insisted on pinning everything down, this or
that, you or me, one or the other. Three of us, for so long
we had been three, none of us could imagine any less.

That flash, flame in the loins, moist rapture – I came first.
Second, Hera: promise, long term. And then, with time, Athena:
wisdom, patience, spinning, building beyond a generation.
We'd worked together as long as any of us could remember.

Then Eris insisted on ranking us. We should have seen it coming.
Divide, conquer. And old Zeus after a few beers never was very swift.
How could they blame the boy? Not even out of his teens,
all he'd known were lambs, that little river, and his mother.

At that age, of course he chose me. And we all three loved him.
Could have settled in easily for the long haul, me with my feathers,
amber honey, Hera's cupboards and shelves, herbs and flannels,
babies, and Athena with her mind like a map, a grid, a star chart,
a proof. She would have organized the entire neighborhood, built

a market square, and the villagers would have filled our temples. We could have made that mountain sing. I tried to make him happy with a woman of his own kind, mortal, but as you know, that backfired.

# Mermaids, the Singing

He leaned over the balcony, let his eyes
touch the edge of sea where birds dipped
in the afternoon, cries across the water.
Pelicans, gulls, not much color.

The mockingbird at home had sung outside
his room every morning, so many songs.
As a boy, he had planned to shoot it
until one day, silence, absence

glaring into the light as he tried
to wake. Maybe he had killed it.
Cried in his room. Never told.
Blurred, the line between sea and sky

out there. At first he thought they were
birds, bobbing on the swells.
He reached for binoculars. Were they women?
And naked? They couldn't be

mermaids. If they were, then under
the water they would stretch
glistening green, silver, quivering
glints of gold as they whipped up foam.

Down the wood steps, across the sand,
he ran.  He could see their heads, hair,
loose.  The surf curled over his ankles.
Arms, pink and dark, pale and brown.

His feet locked on wet sand.  Here
and there a faint crest of a bare
breast and arms pulling toward him.
The salt spray of their splashing.

Waves caught his knees, chest.
The tide rocked him in foam
that frothed the swelling of so
many sudden breasts, round stroking.

So beautiful he thought he'd drown.
But they held him, so many ways
they held him, and he found himself
with every one of them.  He even

swam right up to the oldest, flesh
of her belly rippled as the currents
beyond them.  He shivered as he saw
the chasm of tears between her long

breasts, as she bent down to him,
as he gave her his own tears,
salt water into salt, warm
rocking, the wise cave of her.

When another lifted
nipples like scallops, supple
as if fresh from white shells,
he opened his mouth to her,

dove far into her, with her, through
layers of deeper and deeper water
until he fell back in her arms, asleep.
And woke. Pulled himself, limp,

from the water, dragged himself
over the sand, up the steps
to the evening sky, feathered
with every bird song of this world.

# Annunciations

## 1. The Doves

The day the doves began to roost on her roof.
Their curdled calls, a sound of something boiling.
Odd, the fog that crept so cool, mornings, around the windows,
that by noon cleared for only a couple of hours,
returning mid-afternoon to blanket the house
so the murmuring of the doves seemed louder.

She refilled the feeder that hung
outside the kitchen window. The rush
of tiny kernels of millet into the long tube.
Rush of the small wings of finches, chickadees
landing on the metal rods. When the doves flew down,
smaller birds, frightened, flew away.

Neighbors fussed about the doves, too many,
they tore the roofs. The couple next door trapped them.
Evenings she would creep outside, let the birds loose.
Would come back into the lighted house, finish
the dishes, place them, dripping, into the white drainer
as the doves fluttered into place
under her eaves, settled on her roof, quiet now,
so all she could hear as she slept were the fog horns
calling from the wet black bay, the fog horns,
their low, incessant calling.

## 2. The Owl

In Max Ernst's painting, she is struggling under
the heaviness of a feathery red cape, thousands of
feathers gathered, drifting down from her frail shoulders
like ripples on a dark lake, like the waves
that gripped her in seizures of desire.

Why do her breasts push away from such splendor?
Her nipples harden, refuse to be flattened
under the yoke of this mantle.

Her head has been taken over
by the strange bird. She cannot get away
from the close-set yellow eyes, the way they stare
into the empty tunnels of her body.

## 3. The Swan

It wasn't sudden. She'd been going down
to the pond most evenings, when
the pink flush rose over the water.
The pond had been spilling over its edges, grasses so wet
she was muddy to the thigh now when she walked there,
evenings, as the light changed.

The night he glided to her she wasn't frightened.
Even with the fierce black marks over his eyes.
At first his whiteness barely brushed her legs, but then
every one of his long feathers touched her.

Waking, she slid under
floating pads of lilies, ripples.
The pond opened when she dove down and again
when she lifted white
feathers into the night sky, scattering
stars that pierced the fog.

# III

# WAY OF WHITENESS

# Eclipse

## 1. San Miguel de Allende

Walking to the market for a chicken and carrots
I could barely keep my footing.
Rain flooded cobbles, pulled at the stones
round as eggs, breaking.
Nowhere to walk and stay dry.

On the way down I had driven through forests of yucca,
trees so tall they could barely sustain their own
weight, height, spines bent
to the clay underneath.

When the rain stopped I entered the Church of Carmen,
stone figures filling the chapel, crowded
intricacy of the human knife: faces of angels.
High above, the single father, sword lifted.
Farther down, bleeding feet close to her eyes,
the grown son, stretched beyond suffering.
And between them, the mother, head bent
to her shoulder.

## 2. Assisi

The strange flooding a year ago in July, hot afternoon,
shock of finding my skirt suddenly soaked through
the way it had first happened at twelve.
And the pain, waves of cramping
that would not go away so that all I could think about
was sorrow.

The friends whose lives had swollen
until they cracked open. The woman
whose marriage could not hold, brittle
shell no longer able to contain the yolk
held too long, putrid when it finally broke.
Wet mess, the slippery floor, traitor
to feet exhausted from trying
to keep the shape of the house.

And the friend whose black hair had shone
through a whole concert hall as she played
Liszt, Liszt dances, rhapsodies,
hair braided above her black eyes or
dropping to her spine, falling like a mantle
until the week of the sick headache, until
her head was shaved bald as a stone
and she was gone, her sixteen-year-old son
playing his cello at the service.

The bleeding kept on through the week in Assisi.
I was unable to walk down the hill
to the Basilica of Saint Francis
or even to the nearer Church of Saint Rufino,
its stone Madonna of Tears.


3.  San Antonio

Home by the time of the eclipse,
light under the trees so changed
it could have come from another country.
The stories behind eclipses: punishment from God.
Conjunction of evil with good.
Sun and moon making love.
No longer either/or.  Both/and.
All of it.

Only thing to do is bathe, ease
into water, deep bath under the window under the trees
as the moon moves into the belly of the sun.  At the peak
of the new light's coming,
I step out of the bath, leaving the towel on the rack,
and walk through every room of the house
until outside, I stand under the trees,
drop clean water over the grass
in this umbral light, diffusion
of shadow that will last
only another hour.

# Liquid Poem

It is not true that water has no color.
Nor that milk is white.

During the years I nursed our son,
sometimes when I leaned over you in love

the milk let down and rained
warm over your chest, rippling your hair.

From how far inside it had come.
We could never describe its translucent

clarity, fluidity, digestible sweetness.
And the cologne in this bottle

is lighter than even a petal of jasmine,
easier to smooth

across the inside of my elbow
than anything I know except your mouth.

# At 50, Choosing New Make-Up

The world asks, how are you, and I never know
what to say. A word, a phrase won't do it.
Cosmetics at the counter—bottles, tubes, liquids
to cover the face. Ivory Beige. Tawny Glow. Porcelain Rose.
I could say, I'm fine, I'm Ivory Beige.

Eye makeup I gave up long ago.
The times I used to cry and the mascara
ran black, even when the label said Light
Brown, tunnels staining my cheeks.
Pain of not knowing who I was.

Shopping for skins can drive you wild.
How much does the world need to know?
When my father died I wore the first pink I ever owned.
The folds of the skirt hung in the closet like an azalea, new lips
opening among the dark flannels and tweeds.

If I could decide on one of these shades, cover
the red clusters, broken vessels of my face.
I have found my breathing spaces.
How it feels to look you straight on skin to skin.
This business of artifice

when the ache to connect drives
deeper than it ever did at twenty, the tide rushes
swifter than anyone told you it could. On my hand
veins rise, blue as water from a distance. Rivers
through the body, all that has passed and passed by.

# Practicality, Foam, and Nighties

*Not very practical,* you said, when I brought home
the satiny lace nightie, *won't hold up.* Funny:
this pale shimmer takes to suds as if it were
made for water. Pale green foam

of ocean, pearl bubbles of white lace.
Sometimes when you're floating in the shallows
and a wave folds in, pushes you under,
you gasp at such sudden immersion.

When a breast spills from a slipped strap,
when we sink down under the sheets,
sometimes I would like (wickedly) to whisper
*we are not being very practical.*

# Reason of Lace

Sudden, these cravings
for black lace.  Slips,
nighties, bras of lace

loosed from tight
windings on the spool.
No heaviness of fingers

determined to fold
fabric to a cuff, collar.
Crushed in the palm,

lace reveals nothing
but blackness, stiffness.
Only when loose

across flesh, expanses
of flank, undercurve
of a breast, drifting

over belly, pubis,
does black lace show
its wandering threads,
                mazes of dark

canals, veins, running
vines among the lattice
work of November leaves

that drop, unveil
the further lace of
branches, twigs, intricacy

of the spaces between
thin stems that let
wind shiver

grasses in the field,
sway them as if to music,
the way a hand brushes

the lover's thigh, slowly,
over and over the same
place, yet never the same.

Threads of black
lace like winter
branches stripped to sky

shape regions between
stars, constellations,
pauses in the embroidery

of baroque ornamentation,
exhalation after
a long breath

as the legs begin
their lacing that leads
to the places where fern-

shaped cells spin
gloss, liquid
threads that part,

make way to receive
the small darts that piece
everything together.

# Perennial

We are alone in your car driving across
northern California hills greener than
any I have seen outside of England, yet
we aren't even talking about the green

swimming beyond the windshield, we are
talking of Italy, our love affair
with the Tuscan hills, brown and gold
hills with their spiralling vines,

grapes, and swallows over the olives
shading the red dirt as we sweep
across these green spring hills where
you live with your wife and babies,

you I would have loved if life
had just twisted in another direction,
the way the alley off the main piazza
in Pisa, where you lived the first

year you were married, turned a certain
way, so you learned to find the market
with the open stalls where they sold
the lemon yellow peppers you loved,

the sweet lemon peppers you ate
that year you lived in Pisa. How
you relished them plain, sliced,
whole, steamed, raw, in salads.

The car twists and we crest over
another hill different from the one
back a way and yet the same green.
I loved you once. But never did.

All those years commuting together
and we never touched. Until the night
before I was to move away, with friends
around us in the restaurant, you pressed

your mouth on mine so the shape of
my mouth after that was never the same.
And I love my long-time husband,
and your wife now is, I know, much

better for you than I could have been,
than you would have been for me.
These hills, so many, almost alike,
green after green. Maybe one summer

we'll meet in Italy, maybe we'll rent
a farmhouse with room for our children.
When I go home to my husband, how
can I fit these greens into our car?

I left a winter overcast sky, gray mud.
But now, after flying back, and
driving home, everything here too
as far as I can see has turned green—

lime, moth, juniper, cypress, mesquite
foaming lace over the grasses so soft,
moist, I want to lie down in the field.
And as we talk of the mail that came

while I've been gone, the native sweet
acacia, *huisachillo*, blooms a sudden
start by the road, gold as the little
Tuscan peppers, sweet, crunch, home.

# Inheritance

After my father died, my mother talked of a tree
she had seen at the edge of a field in fall:
a great tree as if on fire, she said, and she wanted
the rest of her life to be like that, one blaze
before the leaves fell, before it all was gone.
Now in the entry near her front door hangs a print
of a winter tree, rounded, heavy, white with snow.

Late winter, you and I have walked this way so often.
I thought I knew what to expect, oaks dropping
their brittle leaves, pushed off by their own buds.
Juniper, scrub. Grasses bent, shadowed with mold.

There is never a way to describe the things that rise
before you. A flush of white straight ahead, a breath
lifting. We turn from the path we'd been following,
into the mud of an abandoned road, to face this scent
of blossom, these circling bees, this bursting:
an old pear, gone back to its wild, original rootstock,
blooming over its intricate branches, a perfect oval.

# Picnic Makings

Fourth grade cafeteria lunches.  If you
brought your own you sat on the floor.
A sea of crowded children.  I'd look inside
my paper bag for the cookies and sandwich:
cheese, or baloney, or peanut butter and
jelly on a good day.  Sucking the last
bit of milk at the bottom of the carton.

✢

When we dated, I would ask him, could we
stop to eat, and he would always say "Sure,
how about here," swing his bright white Healey
into the nearest drive-in.  He'd always be ready
to eat, or cook, and even baked the first time
I stayed with him in his trailer.  Made me
oatmeal raisin cookies, a double recipe.

✢

In Guadalajara my uncle showed us around.
He knew just where to eat, knew the owners.
In the streets he cried, *Look, people
are eating wherever they like, they simply*

*sit down on a curb with their lunch, eat*
*together right here in the square,*
*in Guadalajara it is always a picnic!*

✢

On the train we ate on the pull-down table,
I trimmed green onions with an army knife,
we shared a quiche we had bought in Chartres.
Cherries. We gathered the pits into a kleenex.
The train swayed from side to side, rocking,
we had the whole compartment to ourselves,
and finished two bottles of wine, easy.

✢

South Padre Island, the end of August.
On the sand you hold a spoon to my mouth,
soft white ice cream on the spoon. I take
the cold in my mouth, hold it on my tongue
before I swallow. You put your spoon back
into the cup, offer again, Would you like
some more? Here. Have some more.

# Eating San Gimignano

Towers of gift-wrapped cakes rise
over the counters of the *pasticceria*
across the street from Hotel Bel Soggiorno
where three of us share a room.

Powdered in white sugar, packed
with blanched almonds, hazelnuts,
and honey, these *torte* sell whole.
The old woman whose cheeks

gleam red as roof tiles
will slice them if you like, serve you
a piece of *panforte, mandorlata,*
golden, brown as the towers

that cluster near the center of town.
We have climbed two. We imagine
life in the thirteen hundreds,
what it must have been like

to be a Guelph, building a higher
tower than anyone else, soaring
over the Joneses, the Ghibellines.
From the tallest tower we can peer

down streets that twist
into threads of dark caramel.
Our dinners are included
in the price of our room.

We order à la carte: *tagliarini arrabbiata,*
devil's chicken flaming, sprigged with rosemary,
a bottle of *vernaccia,* and, for a *dolce,*
*tiramisú,* slices of soft cake, layers, white

cheese, whipped cream—"lift me up," it means.
As if eating this much this well
were not adding to luggage
already too heavy

for a fast change of trains.  As if
we are filling only with lightness,
our bellies and buttocks spreading
like summer clouds

billowing over the Tuscan hills
where swallows float
above vineyards, hazy, and dust
sifts like loose sugar

from dry soil, from cracks
between bricks of towers, old
heavy walls, as the evening bells begin
to lift, lift and fill.

# Walking with You

down to the dark lake, lights
clear at last on the other side.

Just enough to see
each other's faces, half a moon.

Something invisible is blooming
into the balm of this spring

darkness. Jasmine?
I haven't seen any.

In the morning, I might find
star jasmine twining

around a palm,
buds bursting in clusters

that open, tonight, our breath.
Or is this perfume roses?

White roses lining the hill, gone
to sogged tissue from the rain,

browned outer layers.  Inner
petals still white, so lush,

scented, they cause all thought
to stop, even as they fall to the path,

almost over now, except for
the swelling hip.  Or perhaps

this sweetness comes from the familiar
shrub by the back door

that has turned to a froth
of cream petals

surrounding a budding seed.
The leaves, strong fingers,

radiate from the blossoming.
I don't know why I am trying to decide

where the scent comes from.
You have taken my hand.
We are walking in the same direction.

# Way of Whiteness

*. . . until the whole field is a*
*white desire, empty, a single stem,*
*a cluster, flower by flower,*
*a pious wish to whiteness gone over. . . .*

—W. C. Williams

All month the moths hovered,
bits and slaps of white pricking
the green mist: yarrow
at Fountains Abbey, dotted blossoms
clustered among leaves and branches, the white
rumps of lazing goats on the hills,
two white horses, muscles
grazing moorland above the Haworth parsonage.

This summer I have been tracking whiteness.
Clusters like doilies, caps, crowns,
but away from our own country
we aren't sure of the names.

You said elderberry, it could have been Queen Anne's Lace.
And on the train the row after row of windows,
one after the other, rhythm of lines
of trees bordering fields, furrows.
The colors friends wore changed daily,

jackets of jade and pink, yellow, green, brilliant
as the crème de menthe at one time
I had thought a fancy drink.

Until this trip I had never had time to walk
behind Chartres, to stop and face the row
of white blooming trees, hawthorns, I finally decided,
masses of white clustering sweet flowers.
Tree after tree, each one almost
as tall as the cathedral.

In Strasbourg on the river blackening one night
someone spotted a swan and suddenly
there were dozens gathered in a cove
of the river, a progression of white neck after
white sliding into the dark.

Miracle of sweet milk in coffee.
Dissolving.
Until, finally at Canterbury, there was only this: white
clouds sweeping behind a spire, the spire
easing into the white
sky filling vision.

And this was even before the music
filled the interior spaces
of the choir at Evensong.

# ACKNOWLEDGMENTS

I wish to thank the editors of the following journals in which earlier versions of these poems first appeared:

*American Literary Review:* "Annunciations" (as "Leda and the Birds"), "Matter of Singing"
*The American Scholar:* "Of Mice and Men," "Perennial"
*The Antioch Review:* "In Venice the Travellers"
*Borderlands:* "Eating San Gimignano," "Inheritance"
*Cafe Solo:* "Olympic Trials"
*Four Quarters:* "Ithaca, On the Landing"
*The Journal:* "Way of Whiteness"
*The Literary Review: An International Quarterly:* "The Face That"
*The North American Review:* "Stylist"
*Poetry:* "Color Analysis," "Reason of Lace," "Taking a Language"
*RiverSedge:* "Some Days the Only"
*Spoon River Poetry Review:* "Liquid Poem"
*Tar River Poetry:* "The Bottom"

I am especially grateful to the Rockefeller Foundation and the University of Texas at San Antonio for time to complete this manuscript.

I am deeply grateful to friends, particularly David Dooley, Christine Leche, and Jeannine Keenan, as well as Laurence Barker, who helped to see the poems of this collection through a variety of stages.

# ABOUT THE AUTHOR

Wendy Barker is the author of two previous volumes of poetry, *Winter Chickens* and *Let the Ice Speak*, and a chapbook, *Eve Remembers*. As a critic she is the author of *Lunacy of Light: Emily Dickinson and the Experience of Metaphor* and coeditor (with Sandra M. Gilbert) of *The House Is Made of Poetry: The Art of Ruth Stone*. She has received grants from the National Endowment for the Arts and the Rockefeller Foundation, and she has published widely in journals, including *Poetry, The American Scholar, North American Review, Michigan Quarterly Review, Prairie Schooner,* and *Ontario Review*. She lives in San Antonio, Texas, and is a professor of English at the University of Texas at San Antonio.

*Photograph by John Poindexter*

# COLOPHON

Seven hundred copies of *Way of Whiteness*, by Wendy Barker, have been printed on 70 pound Filare "crema ivory paper, containing fifty percent recycled fiber and 25 percent cotton, by Williams Printing & Graphics of San Antonio, Texas. Text and poem titles were set in Garamond 3 type, book and section titles in Caslon Openface type.

*Way of Whiteness* was entirely designed and produced by Bryce Milligan, publisher, Wings Press, incorporating the design preferences of the poet.

The first twenty-five copies off the press were numbered, signed, and dated by the author.

Wings Press was founded in 1975 by J. Whitebird and Joseph F. Lomax as "an informal association of artists and cultural mythologists dedicated to the preservation of the literature of the nation of Texas." The current publisher/editor is honored to carry on that mission and expand it to include fine writing from all over the Americas.

## Recent and Forthcoming Poetry
## from Wings Press

*Way of Whiteness* by Wendy Barker (Spring 2000)

*Burnt Water Suite* by Darrell Bourque (1999)

*Hook & Bloodline* by Chip Dameron (Spring 2000)

*Peace in the Corazón* by Victoria García-Zapata (1999)

*Cande, te estoy llamando* by Celeste Guzmán (1999)

*Winter Poems from Eagle Pond* by Donald Hall (1999)

*Strong Box Heart* by Sheila Sánchez Hatch (Spring 2000)

*Seven Cigarette Story* by Courtenay Martin (1999)

*Mama Yetta and Other Poems* by Hermine Pinson (1999)

*Smolt* by Nicole Pollentier (1999)

*Long Story Short* by Mary Grace Rodríguez (1999)

*Garabato Poems* by Virgil Suárez (1999)

*Sonnets to Human Beings* by Carmen Tafolla (1999)

*Sonnets and Salsa* by Carmen Tafolla (Spring 2000)

*Finding Peaches in the Desert* by Pam Uschuk (Spring 2000

*Vida* by Alma Luz Villanueva (Fall 2000)